GREAT ZOMBIES
IN HISTORY

T0048134

Contributions to Zombie Studies

White Zombie: Anatomy of a Horror Film. Gary D. Rhodes. 2001

The Zombie Movie Encyclopedia. Peter Dendle. 2001

American Zombie Gothic: The Rise and Fall (and Rise) of the Walking Dead in Popular Culture. Kyle William Bishop. 2010

Back from the Dead: Remakes of the Romero Zombie Films as Markers of Their Times. Kevin J. Wetmore, Jr. 2011

Generation Zombie: Essays on the Living Dead in Modern Culture. Edited by Stephanie Boluk and Wylie Lenz. 2011

Race, Oppression and the Zombie: Essays on Cross-Cultural Appropriations of the Caribbean Tradition. Edited by Christopher M. Moreman and Cory James Rushton. 2011

Zombies Are Us: Essays on the Humanity of the Walking Dead. Edited by Christopher M. Moreman and Cory James Rushton. 2011

The Zombie Movie Encyclopedia, Volume 2: 2000–2010. Peter Dendle. 2012

Great Zombies in History. Edited by Joe Sergi. 2013 (graphic novel)

Unraveling Resident Evil: *Essays on the Complex Universe of the Games and Films.* Edited by Nadine Farghaly. 2014

"We're All Infected": Essays on AMC's The Walking Dead *and the Fate of the Human.* Edited by Dawn Keetley. 2014

Zombies and Sexuality: Essays on Desire and the Walking Dead. Edited by Shaka McGlotten and Steve Jones. 2014

GREAT ZOMBIES in HISTORY

EDITED BY JOE SERGI

FOREWORD BY ARNOLD T. BLUMBERG

CONTRIBUTIONS TO ZOMBIE STUDIES

McFarland & Company, Inc., Publishers
Jefferson, North Carolina

Acknowledgments: This book would not be possible without the work of: Rob Anderson, who was the original project manager and editor of the individual stories. Without Rob's hard work and dedication, this book would not exist. Frederick Kim and George O'Connor, who served as Associate Editors on the Project. E.T. Dollman, who prepared the logo and design for the book.

Library of Congress Cataloguing-in-Publication Data

Great zombies in history / edited by Joe Sergi ; foreword by Arnold T. Blumberg.
    p.   cm.— (Contributions to Zombie Studies)

ISBN 978-0-7864-7456-1
softcover : acid free paper ∞

1. Zombies—History.   I. Sergi, Joe, 1970–
GR581.G74 2013   398.21—dc23   2013015664

British Library cataloguing data are available

© 2013 Joe Sergi. All rights reserved

No part of this book may be reproduced or transmitted in any form or by any means, electronic or mechanical, including photocopying or recording, or by any information storage and retrieval system, without permission in writing from the publisher.

On the cover: Art by Dafu Yu and Colors by Paolo Chaz Gomez.

Printed in the United States of America

McFarland & Company, Inc., Publishers
Box 611, Jefferson, North Carolina 28640
www.mcfarlandpub.com

To George, father of the zombie apocalypse.

And to Robert, Max, and all the other children who keep the war going and the dead walking.

CONTENTS

FOREWORD

Zombies may be more popular than ever, but they remain a monster rooted firmly in modern times. A late addition to the pop culture pantheon introduced via films like *White Zombie* (1932) and *I Walked with a Zombie* (1943) after the publication of William Seabrook's skewed and sensationalistic 1929 report on Voudoun in the West Indies, *The Magic Island*, the zombie has gone through quite a strange evolution over the years.

Now largely thought of as reanimated corpses on the lookout for a buffet of living flesh, zombies have infiltrated every medium and continue to spread across the globe. Countries like Greece and Pakistan have produced their first zombie movies in the last few years, the creatures are regularly shambling — or running, let's be inclusive — across screens both big and small, and it seems that when it comes to a good zombie apocalypse we can't help enjoying the utter collapse of everything we know and cherish. Board up the doors and windows, lock and load, leave the radio on and let the good times — and perhaps heads — roll.

But although we love the living dead, we tend to keep them corralled to just one time and place. Not just because of its function as a metaphor for the unraveling of our civilization but as a dark reflection of ourselves and all the

things we most fear, the zombie — more than any other monster — seems to fit best in a present-day, urban environment. The cities are crumbling, the military is no help at all, and the politicians have run for the hills as the moaning corpses march on; it's just like we always knew it would be.

That's all well and good — sort of — but isn't there some fun to be had in giving the vampires, werewolves, and mummies a break and letting the zombies loose in history? What about the Revolutionary War? How about Man's first journey into space? Feudal Japan? Xerxes' Fightin' 300? But it's not just about a fresh take on a moldering army of corpses laying siege to society; there's meaning in the madness whenever and wherever zombies strike.

History teaches us many things, not least our tendency to make the same mistakes over and over again. For all of our accomplishments, Mankind's hold on this world is a fragile one, precariously balanced between order and chaos at any given moment. All it takes is one precipitating event to consign entire civilizations to dust, and when you look at centuries of recorded history, you see that same story play out with alarming consistency.

Why add zombies to that equation? Like so much of our entertainment, horror offers a way to safely gaze into the abyss. The zombie serves a vital purpose, giving us a chance to stare directly into the cold, cloudy eyes of our own worst fears. And when the credits roll, you can leave the darkness of your local movie theater, walk out into the sunlight of a new day, and leave those fears behind…at least for a little while.

So when cracking those history books only reveals to you that our modern, iPhone-toting, Internet-using, Starbucks-drinking society is little more than a house of cards, a civilized culture one disaster away from feral anarchy, you might need the cushion of a cathartic metaphor to make the message a bit more palatable. Yes, the world outside your door is collapsing, but it's not really happening; it's just the return of the living dead.

Add zombies to history and stir. There they are, our distorted carnival mirror image, stalking through time, accompanying us on our march from past to future. They are always with us; they are us, so why shouldn't they turn up everywhere from ancient Greece to 1700s America?

After all, they belong there.

Arnold T. Blumberg

*Arnold T. Blumberg is an author, book designer, educator, former museum curator, and internationally recognized zombie expert. He co-authored **Zombiemania: 80 Movies to Die For**, contributed to **Triumph of the Walking Dead** and **Braaaiiinnnsss! From Academics to Zombies**, and teaches a course in zombies in popular media at the University of Baltimore.*

IMMORTAL RESISTANCE

For several days in 480 BC, at the narrow pass known as Thermopylae, 300 Spartan warriors and other Greek soldiers under the command of King Leonidas fought to block the progress of King Xerxes and his massive Persian army.

Ancient scholars claimed that the legendary "300" faced millions of Persian soldiers, but modern historians scoff at that number due to the unlikely logistics of supporting such a large military force.

But what if Xerxes' army really did number in the millions ... and needed no rest ... and no water ... as they shambled forward to battle?

Writer
Rob Anderson

Artist
DaFu Yu

Letterer
E.T. Dollman

...BECAUSE ONLY AN *IRON WILL* CAN STAND SHOULDER-TO-SHOULDER IN THE FACE OF THE *UNDEAD HORDE.*

XERXES CALLED HIS GUARD "THE IMMORTALS" FOR A REASON. AN ARMY THAT NEEDS NO FOOD OR WATER CAN MARCH ENDLESSLY.

WE NUMBERED 300 AND FACED AN ARMY OF TWO MILLION... LIVING AND DEAD. AN INCONCEIVABLE NUMBER.

OUR TASK WAS SIMPLE. HOLD THE PASS. GIVE THE GREEK PENINSULA TIME TO PREPARE.

STILL, WE DID NOT WANT TO DIE.

BUT I HAD A PLAN TO DELAY THEM ONE LAST DAY.

I AM LOATH TO ADMIT THIS, UNCLE LEONIDAS, BUT I AM SICK WITH DREAD.

I UNDERSTAND MORE THAN YOU KNOW, ALPHEOS. BUT YOUR KING NEEDS YOUR COURAGE *TONIGHT*. WILL YOU HELP ME PREPARE?

Y-YES, OF COURSE! BUT I DON'T KNOW WHAT I CAN—

BEFORE WE DEPARTED LACEDAEMON, THE ORACLES WARNED ME OF THE SICKNESS. HOW IT PRESERVES AND STRENGTHENS THE BODY, BUT DESTROYS THE MIND.

I BELIEVE I CAN HARNESS ITS POWER.

IF THE SICKNESS OVERCOMES THE MIND DUE TO FEAR...

...I WILL NOT BEND TO IT.

UUUURRHH...

UNCLE, NO!

URRGGH!

GROMMPHH

6

7

THE BATTLE RESUMED. TIME WAS MEASURED IN A MILLION SLASHES AND CUTS. DID THE END COME IN HOURS? IN MINUTES?

WE SLAUGHTERED MORE THAN 20,000 PERSIANS... LIVING AND DEAD. MANY THOUSANDS, I KILLED WITH MY OWN SWORD.

AT THE LAST, I SAW ALPHEOS FIGHTING WITH TOOTH AND NAIL.

HE FACED HIS FEAR LIKE A SPARTAN.

AND, AS FOR ME, WHATEVER I HAD BECOME...

...I WAS STILL ONLY ONE AGAINST THE HORDE.

XERXES TOOK HIS REVENGE UPON ME, AND MY DAYS OF BATTLE ENDED ABRUPTLY.

NO BOUNTY HERE

In AD 986, Erik the Red, a famous Viking leader, wanted to draw others to a land he had discovered after being exiled from Iceland.

He wisely called this land "Greenland" to lure potential settlers there, promising fertile land and resources to exploit.

History tells us that some Vikings reached Greenland and settled there. It has always been a bit of a mystery as to why their settlements did not endure and why they lost contact with their homelands for so many years.

It is suspected that the Vikings were not alone...

Writer
Neil Fisher

Artist
Derek Chase

Inker
David Strosnider

Letterer
Christian Ruiz

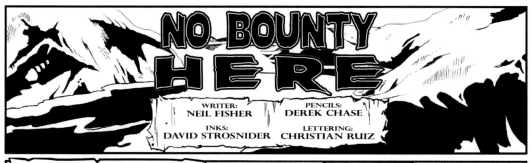

NO BOUNTY HERE

WRITER: NEIL FISHER   **PENCILS:** DEREK CHASE

INKS: DAVID STROSNIDER   **LETTERING:** CHRISTIAN RUIZ

GREENLAND AD 986: FOUR VIKING SURVIVORS OF A SHIPWRECK LOOK TO SETTLE THIS NEW LAND. HOWEVER, THEY ARE NOT ALONE.

HO! WE SEEK FOOD AND SHELTER! DO YOU UNDERSTAND?

< LOOK AT THEIR WEAPONS! THEY COME TO ATTACK US!>

YOU *DON'T* WANT TO DO THIS, LITTLE MAN.

THE NEXT MORNING

〈THIS IS MADNESS!〉

〈WOULD YOU HAVE ME DO NOTHING?〉

EARLY THAT NIGHT.

〈RISE, TUPILAQ, RISE! AVENGE MY SON!〉

TWO HOURS LATER...

14

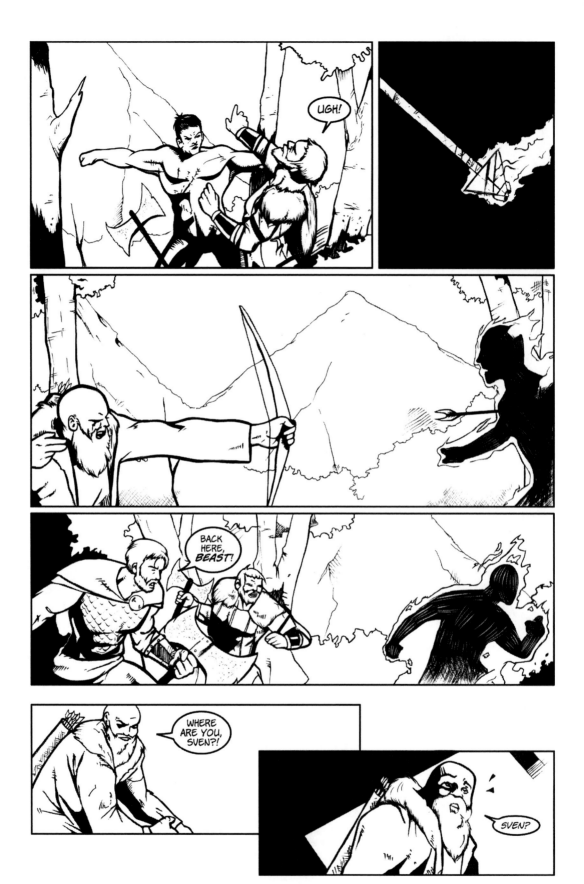

17

ENOUGH OF THIS!

〈HA, HA, HA!〉

〈HA, HA, HA!〉

〈NOOOO!〉

THIS ENDS NOW, HELLSPAWN!

A LAND OF PLENTY, WE WERE TOLD. AND ALL FOR NAUGHT.

BAH! LET THIS SERVE AS A WARNING.

THERE IS NO BOUNTY HERE!

BUSHIDO

The samurai of feudal Japan valued honor and loyalty above all. Under Bushido, their code of conduct, samurai would rather die than bear the shame of defeat.

During the Sengoku Period, also known as the "Period of Warring Kingdoms," internal conflicts and Western encroachment escalated the violence.

One of these conflicts, the Onin War, saw the Hosokawa and Yamana clans clash in the hills of Kyoto.

Though the war would last for 11 years, this story tells the tale of one particularly strange day out of many bloody ones...

Writer
Eric Drumm

Artist
Leandro Panganiban

Letterer
Travis Lanham

KYOTO, JAPAN - 1468

BUSHIDO

WHERE *ARE* THEY? THESE BASTARDS NOT ONLY ENCROACH ON OUR TRADE, BUT THEY ARE LATE AS WELL.

AND TO THINK, I POLISHED MY ARMOR FOR THIS CIRCUS. SHAMEFUL.

DON'T WORRY. ONCE THEY ARRIVE, I'LL BE SPRAYING YOU WITH THEIR *BLOOD*, KIYOSHI.

REMAIN *DISCIPLINED.*

ARE YOU THAT ANXIOUS FOR A FIGHT, KENTARO?

YOU HAVE *NO* IDEA.

I THINK WE ARE IN THE WRONG PLACE...

WELL, *THAT'S* EMBARRASSING.

ENOUGH! EVERYONE OVER THE HILL! *NOW!*

21

AKIRA! WE NEED A NEW BATTLE PLAN!

KILL THE NEXT THING THAT COMES NEAR YOU.

AGREED.

DO YOU WANT TO GO TO HELL WITHOUT ANY *STORIES* TO TELL?

SHUNK

26

I AM... UNCLEAN. I CANNOT CONTINUE.

KIYOSHI...

DON'T.

I INTEND TO DIE WITH *HONOR.*

WILL YOU HONOR ME BY ASSISTING, MY FRIEND?

OF COURSE.

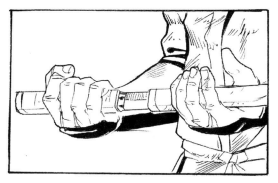

27

CRO

On July 22, 1587, 117 British settlers landed on Roanoke Island. Soon after their arrival, natives killed one of the settlers while he was away from the rest of the colony.

Fearing for their lives, the settlers asked Governor John White to return to England to ask for help. Due to the Anglo-Spanish War, White was unable to return to Roanoke for three years.

When he arrived on August 18, 1590, there was no sign that the colony had ever existed. All that was left were the letters "CRO" carved into a tree. White was at a loss to explain the disappearance.

How had the colony been completely erased from the land and history?

Writer
George O'Connor

Artist
Eric Carter

Special thanks to Amy Fletcher and Tracy O'Connor.

29

I had been told to watch them and so I did for 23 moons.

How I laughed at them.

So clumsy. So disconnected from the world around them.

They didn't know how to listen to the land.

They didn't notice when the animals stopped talking.

They didn't notice when the animals started leaving.

When **I** noticed, it was too late.

31

I tried to warn them.

The men laughed at the dancing savage.

The women shrieked at the half-naked tan man.

The children were just curious and came closer.

Then...

...everyone was screaming.

We were taught at an early age that when caught by surprise, running equaled survival.

These people were taught to fight an enemy.

So they tried.

These **things** were their fathers, sons and husbands who left days ago to explore the land.

The innocents had no idea what they were up against. This wasn't a European problem...yet.

As I ran, I could hear the screams rise...

...then stop.

One...

...by...

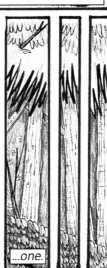

...one.

33

When I returned with my people...

...I prayed we would still hear crying or screaming.

That would mean life.

Instead we heard ripping...

...and tearing.

The sound of creatures unaware that they had already died.

34

We cleansed the land...

...the way our ancestors taught us.

We dismantled their village and gathered the fallen...

...and burned it all.

Later, I decided that I was no longer worthy of acting as scout.

The name my people had for this land has been lost to history.

It became known as...

ROANOKE ISLAND

THE GRAY AND THE PALE

In the spring of 1804, the famed expedition of Lewis and Clark ventured west toward the Pacific Ocean seeking to make a firm claim on discovery of the Pacific Northwest.

This journey was important for several reasons. They wished to map out the waterways for commercial use as well as to compete with the British for control of land and the fur trade.

A year later, they met Toussaint Charbonneau and his wife, a Shoshone named Sacajawea. She proved to be vital to the expedition as an interpreter and a guide.

This is an account of how she saved the expedition from an unspeakable horror and helped alter the history of this continent.

Writer
Dan Rivera

Artist & Letterer
Richard P. Clark

May, 1805

The Missouri River

When my husband told me we were leaving with Captain Lewis, I was upset he picked me instead of his other wife.

I always get taken away from my home. First the Hidasa Tribe took me from my family and now this fur trapper.

The storm came suddenly and my husband was as terrible at steering a pirogue as he was at being a gentleman.

I was able to save Captain Clark's maps and personal journal, but was not able to save our supply of berries and nuts.

Thankfully our infant son was safe on board another pirogue.

AAAH!!

Damn it, Charbonneau you useless frog!

Campbell, are you all right?

I think something bit me!

Poor Campbell became very ill. Captain Lewis was the closest thing we had to a doctor, so he wanted to treat him.

You think you are important because you saved Clark's papers?

You are *my* wife, not *his*.

Stop... please.

Waaaaah!

Don't forget that.

Waaah!

I've never seen a bite like that. It looked... *human*.

There was *something* 'bout that water, Clark. Felt like there was some evil in it.

He's gone. I couldn't stop the infection and the fever.

Lewis, we have a guest.

The woman was Kimama, a Shoshone like myself. She left her village to look for her missing son.

She talked about how this land was cursed, and how she fears that the "Gray" have taken him. She had been lucky to avoid them so far.

"The gray?" Captain Lewis asked.

Kimama said that there are those who live between the physical and the spirit worlds.

Creatures without reason that only crave flesh...

...especially the flesh of the pale.

44

Cut off their *heads!*

There are those who would say that the Gray's presence is the land fighting back against the White man...

BLAM!

But the child on my back is **mine,** and I will **not** lose him to **this.**

THWACK!

I see a chance for **freedom** in front of me.

Aidez-moi!

But I choose **another** path.

I should have **let** them eat you.

THWISSSSH!

The battle was won, although I am curious at how this story will be told.

<My child... do not let me join the gray.>

<Beware of the pale... they are... evil. Please... make sure I enter the Land of the Coyote... so I may be with my son.>

<I promise.>

SSSHLLLK...

Kimama was right. I reunited with my family later, when the Expedition was desperate for horses.

I can only hope that she was reunited with her son as well.

THE ZOMBIE WAR OF 1812

In the 38 year period since the United States declared independence, the fledgling country had seen the birth of democracy and the death of its first President, George Washington.

Unfortunately, diplomatic relations with Great Britain worsened and, in 1812, America declared war. On August 14, 1814, troops led by British General Robert Ross invaded Washington, D.C., and set fire to many government buildings.

Only the quick thinking of the First Lady, Dolley Madison, saved the treasures in the White House, including the Presidential portrait of George Washington.

At least that is the official story.

Writer
Joe Sergi

Artist
Marc Jameson

Letterer
E.T. Dollman

The ZOMBIE WAR of 1812

Writer
JOE SERGI

Artist
MARC JAMESON

Letterer
E.T. DOLLMAN

We heard rumors of the creatures on the road, but only isolated incidents.

Then stories came about undead soldiers gathering into a larger group near Lexington.

The unorganized mob moved in a slow mass on the road to Virginia, which is where the monsters faced General Ross and his troops. If we hadn't arrived to cover Ross's retreat, I fear all would have been lost.

ENGAGE THE ENEMY!

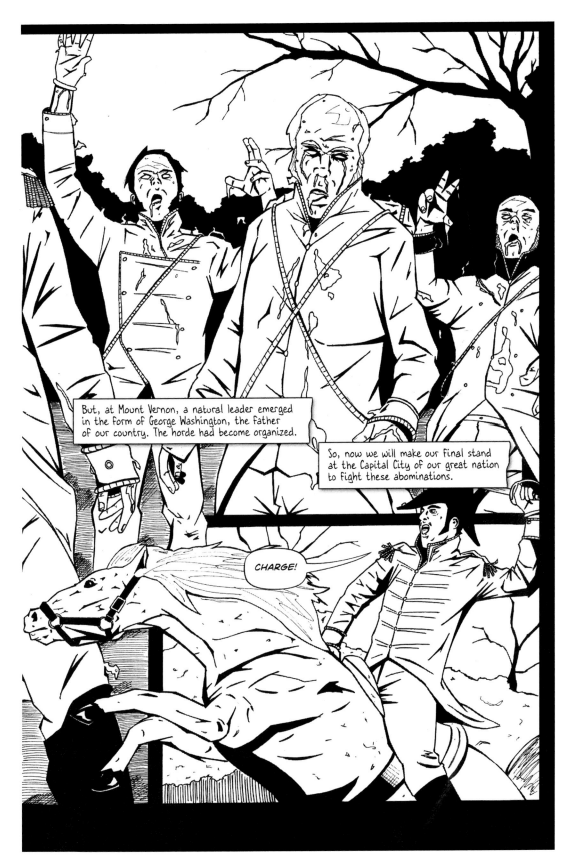

54

55

THE DEAD & ENDLESS WASTES

While Teddy Roosevelt genuinely loved the years he spent ranching in the Bad Lands of the Dakota Territory, the winter of 1884–1885 was a particularly bleak time for him, due to the recent deaths of both his wife and mother.

His mood colored his outlook, and he wrote about the world he inhabited using such descriptions as "lifeless silence," "like the shadow of silent death," and "dead and endless wastes."

Roosevelt's spirit was ultimately irrepressible, however. This story is a fanciful account of how he went from being a person in mourning to the man Stephen Ambrose summarized thusly: "So much pleasure did he take in living that he is best described as pure joy."

Writer & Letterer
Frederick Kim

Artist
Antonio Bifulco

THE DEAD & ENDLESS WASTES

STORY & LETTERS - FREDERICK KIM
ART - ANTONIO BIFULCO

DAKOTA TERRITORY, 1884

ANOTHER ONE, MR. ROOSEVELT. THOUGH I CAN'T TELL IF IT'S ONE OF OURS...

THEODORE ROOSEVELT, AGE 26.

GIVEN ITS CURRENT STATE, GEORGE--

--IT WOULD BE DIFFICULT TO NAME ITS SPECIES, MUCH LESS WHICH RANCH IT CAME FROM!

GOT TO BE A PACK OF WOLVES. OR MOUNTAIN LIONS, MAYBE.

PERHAPS.

I DON'T BOTHER TELLING GEORGE THIS WASN'T THE WORK OF WOLVES OR LIONS. WE BOTH KNOW NEITHER ANIMAL WALKS ON *TWO FEET*.

WHATEVER MADE THESE TRACKS IS SOMETHING NEITHER OF US HAS DEALT WITH BEFORE.

WE RIDE ON IN SILENCE, OUR THOUGHTS AND PREMONITIONS BETTER LEFT UNSPOKEN.

AND THE HARSH DESOLATION OF THIS LAND SETTLES INTO THE DARKNESS AT THE VERY HEART OF ME, ONCE AGAIN.

HOW I MISS YOU, MY DEAR, SWEET, ALICE.

I KNOW RIGHT AWAY THERE'S SOMETHING VERY WRONG, WHEN WE SEE THE FIRST ONE IN THE CENTER OF THE RAVINE.

IT'S HIS APPEARANCE, AND THE WAY THE ELEMENTS DON'T TROUBLE HIM, DESPITE HIS LACK OF WINTER DRESS.

GRRARRGHH...

DEAR GOD. IS THAT A...A MAN?

I DOUBT IT, GEORGE. AT LEAST, NOT *ANYMORE*.

HE'S BEEN... *CHANGED*, IN SOME MANNER.

THE PROOF IS DELIVERED WHEN THE MONSTROSITY ATTACKS US.

SHOTS THAT WOULD HAVE DROPPED A *GRIZZLY* HAVE NO EFFECT ON IT.

BOOM!

BLAM!

ONLY WHEN I AIM FOR ITS HEAD DOES THE CREATURE FINALLY SUCCUMB.

61

63

65

RESCUED BY THE RIPPER?

Jack the Ripper is the first modern serial killer. His violent murders of Whitechapel prostitutes in the late 1800s remain the subject of much discussion and debate.

Who was he? What motivated him to cut the throats of prostitutes? Why did he remove the internal organs of his victims before mutilating their bodies?

The killings inexplicably ceased on November 9, 1888.

The reason why remains a mystery.

Until now...

Writer
Joshua Osborne

Artist
Randy Valiente

Letterer
E.T. Dollman

WHITECHAPEL, LONDON. 1888.

WHEN FISHING, BAIT IS REQUIRED TO ATTRACT THE FISH TO YOUR HOOK. LURES, WORMS, WHATEVER WORKS BEST FOR YOU.

RESCUED BY THE RIPPER?

Written by
JOSHUA OSBORNE
Illustrated by
RANDY VALIENTE
Lettered by
E.T. DOLLMAN

WHEN STALKING JACK THE RIPPER, THERE IS NO BETTER BAIT THAN A FEMALE PROSTITUTE.

HE'S BEEN KILLING FOR WEEKS NOW, EVADING EVERY ATTEMPT THAT SCOTLAND YARD HAS MADE TO CAPTURE HIM.

MANY OF THE WOMEN I ONCE CALLED FRIENDS ARE GONE NOW.

TAKE HER, FOR INSTANCE. THIS IS DOROTHY, AND SHE'LL SOON BE DEAD.

BUT IT'S OK... SHE'S A REAL BITCH.

THIS ISN'T ABOUT REVENGE THOUGH. THIS IS ABOUT SELF-PRESERVATION. EVERY PROSTITUTE IN THE WHITECHAPEL AREA HAS A TARGET ON HER BACK UNTIL HE'S FOUND.

SO I MADE IT MY MISSION TO FIND THE RIPPER...

BEFORE HE FOUND ME...

67

I'LL EXPLAIN ONCE WE GET TO MY SECRET HIDEOUT.

YOU HAVE A SECRET HIDEOUT?

OF COURSE I DO! JUST SIT TIGHT. WE'LL BE THERE IN A FEW MINUTES.

THE SEWERS OF WHITECHAPEL, A FEW MINUTES LATER.

WHAT'S WITH THE CAULDRON? AND WHO WAS THAT MAN YOU KILLED EARLIER?

THAT MAN WAS NOTHING MORE THAN A MERE COPYCAT KILLER.

SOMEBODY WANTING THE FAME AND PUBLICITY OF JACK THE RIPPER, WITHOUT HAVING PUT IN ALL THE HARD WORK.

HIS FIRST AND ONLY KILL CAME TONIGHT.

OW.

AS FOR THE CAULDRON, I'VE BEEN HARVESTING THE ORGANS OF MY VICTIMS IN ORDER TO PREPARE AN ELIXIR THAT MAY BE ABLE TO SAVE THE WORLD.

BUT THAT CAN'T HAPPEN UNLESS YOU DO ME A FAVOR...

MY "ZOMBIE CURSE", AS I'VE HEARD OTHERS REFER TO IT, CAN ONLY BE LIFTED BY A KISS FROM MY TRUE LOVE... YOU!

A KISS...

WITH TONGUE...

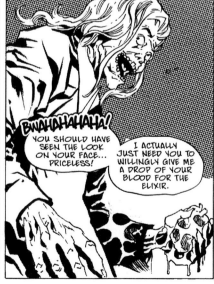

BWAHAHAHAHA! YOU SHOULD HAVE SEEN THE LOOK ON YOUR FACE... PRICELESS!

I ACTUALLY JUST NEED YOU TO WILLINGLY GIVE ME A DROP OF YOUR BLOOD FOR THE ELIXIR.

YOU ARE AN ASS!

GUILTY.

WHAT ARE YOU TRYING TO SAVE THE WORLD FROM? AND WHY MY BLOOD?

MANY YEARS AGO, A PLAGUE SWEPT ACROSS THE LAND AND KILLED MOST OF THOSE THAT BECAME INFECTED.

THOSE THAT DIDN'T DIE TURNED INTO WHAT YOU SEE BEFORE YOU.

I'VE PREDICTED A SIMILAR PLAGUE WILL ONCE AGAIN SPREAD ACROSS THE LAND.

BUT THE ELIXIR CALLS FOR THE BLOOD OF A WILLING HUMAN BEING AND I FIGURED THERE'S NO ONE MORE WILLING THAN A PROSTITUTE.

THAT'S WHY YOU'VE BEEN KILLING PROSTITUTES?

YES, BUT ONLY BECAUSE THEY WERE TOO AFRAID TO HELP ME. WHY AREN'T YOU?

WHY AM I NOT AFRAID OF YOU? I'M A WHORE. I'VE SLEPT WITH UGLIER MEN THAN YOU.

ARE YOU COMING ON TO ME?

NOT A CHANCE.

SO I JUST CUT MYSELF AND LET THE BLOOD DROP INTO THE CAULDRON?

YEAH, AND AT THAT SAME TIME I'LL DROP THE HEART IN AS WELL.

OK, LET'S GET THIS OVER WITH.

3

2

1

GO!

SPLASH!

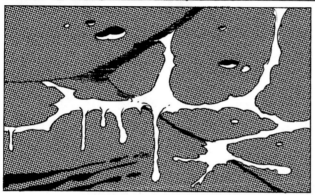

END

THE MOTHERLAND KNOWS

The lure of space has captivated our species for its entire existence. Not content merely to look at the stars, we dreamed of how to conquer them.

Prior to sending the first humans into space, scientists around the world studied the rigors of space travel by sending animals into orbit. Although many died, most returned unharmed.

Soviet cosmonaut Yuri Gagarin made history when he became the first human being in space during his Earth orbit on April 12th, 1961 aboard Vostok 1. He returned safely to Earth and became an instant international celebrity.

However, as humanity broke beyond the edge of their planet and took their first steps into space, they found something quite disturbing...

Writer
Kevin D. Lintz

Artist
Leandro Panganiban

Letterer
Kevin D. Lintz

THE MOTHERLAND ★ KNOWS

WRITER:
KEVIN D. LINTZ

ARTIST:
LEANDRO PANGANIBAN

LETTERING:
KEVIN D. LINTZ

Star City, Moscow,
Soviet Union

13 April 1961

One day after the landing, it is clear that even though our predictions were correct, the situation is more complicated than we expected.
He is uncontrollable.

The animals which returned from orbit showed increased aggression, enhanced intelligence, and a terrible hunger.

We felt certain that we could contain a human subject.

We miscalculated. Yuri is so angry.

CRASH!

WHAT HAVE YOU DONE TO ME?!?

M-M-MAJOR GAGARIN, PLEASE...

YOU KNEW THIS WOULD HAPPEN, DIDN'T YOU?

YOU WERE READY WHEN I RETURNED!

IT WAS A POSSIBILITY, BUT W-WE WEREN'T CERTAIN.

YOU LIE!!

AAIIIGGGHHH!

SKLUSCH!

WELL, WHAT NOW, MY FRIENDS?

FOLLOWING YURI GAGARIN'S HISTORIC FLIGHT, THE UNITED STATES IS POISED TO SEND ITS OWN "ASTRONAUT" INTO ORBIT.

THE WHOLE WORLD WATCHED THE SOVIETS SEND THEIR HERO, GAGARIN, INTO SPACE.

WELL, THE GOOD OL' USA ISN'T GOING TO BE OUTDONE, NOT BY A LONG SHOT!

Alan Shepard to launch into space next week.

TV.

OF COURSE...

WE WILL GO TO JOIN OUR BROTHER WHEN HE RETURNS.

HE WILL BE ANGRY, TOO.

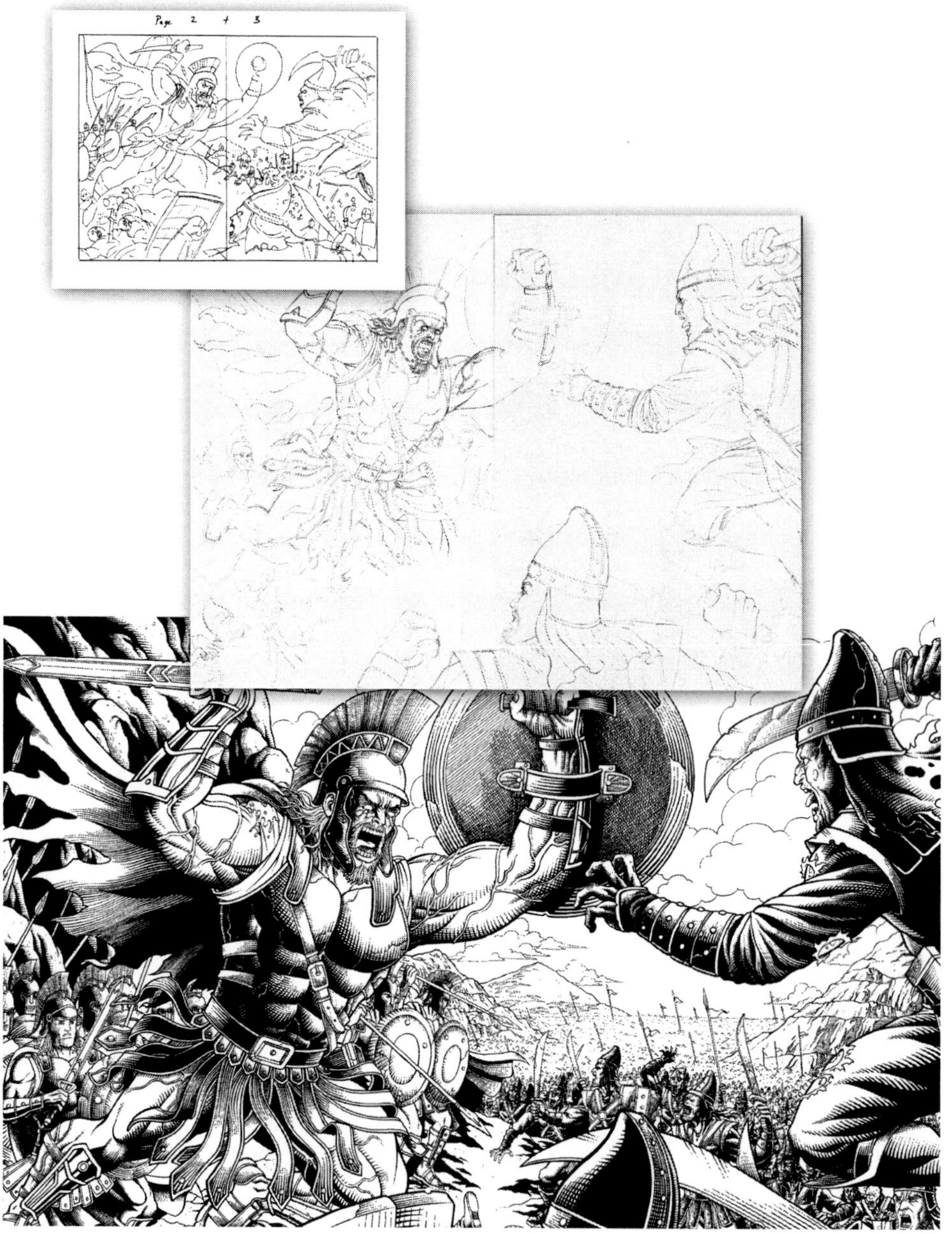
Page 2 + 3

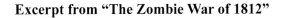

Excerpt from "The Zombie War of 1812"

Panel One:

Establishing shot: A military camp circa 1818. (See photo reference A from Williamsburg, VA.) Men are gathered outside the tents cooking over fires, cleaning weapons, and playing instruments. One man in a general's uniform (see photo reference B of Andrew Jackson) is writing a letter.

Caption 1

(NOTE TO LETTERER the text in the caption should be in a script-type font as this is a letter home)

August 24, 1814, Bladensburg, Maryland.

My dearest wife Rachel, I apologize for my lapse in correspondence. I know you must be worried sick that I have not written you since our battle at Horseshoe Bend.

Panel Two:

General William Henry Harrison (see photo reference C) overlooks a map of Washington DC with small markers on it (think the Stratego game board). The general is dressed in an American uniform. Two soldiers flank him, looking at the map. They are inside a tent with the opening of the tent behind them.

Caption 2:

As you know from my previous correspondence, my Seventh Military District army has joined General Harrison's Brigade in our effort to stop the advances of General Robert Ross and his British forces.

Soldier 3:

General Harrison, we await your orders.

General Harrison 4:

There is no alternative. Our course is set.

Panel Three:

Same Panel Two except now General Robert Ross dressed in a British soldier's uniform (see photo reference D) is in the entranceway to the tent.

Caption 5:

Circumstances have changed and now we stand on the cusp of an even greater threat to our fledgling nation.

General Harrison 6:

General Ross, what is the situation?

Panel Four:

Close up of General Ross. He looks grim.

Caption 7:

A threat that has made allies of enemies.

General Ross 8:

General Harrison, the enemy force has amassed in Alexandria, outside the border. Our troops stand ready to engage.

General Ross 9:

It is time.

Panel Five:

General Harrison reaches for his sword hanging on a post. He has a determined but grim look.

Caption 10:

And requires that we sacrifice all that we have fought so hard to build.

General Harrison 11:

Then, may God have mercy on us all.

Bushido

Art by Leandro Panganiban

Bushido
Art by Leandro Panganiban

Bushido
Art by Leandro Panganiban

Immortal Resistance
Art by DaFu Yu

Persian Zombie Warrior

Immortal Resistance
Art by DaFu Yu

Immortal Resistance
Art by DaFu Yu

The Motherland Knows
Art by Leandro Panganiban

The Motherland Knows
Art by Leandro Panganiban

The Motherland Knows
Art by Leandro Panganiban

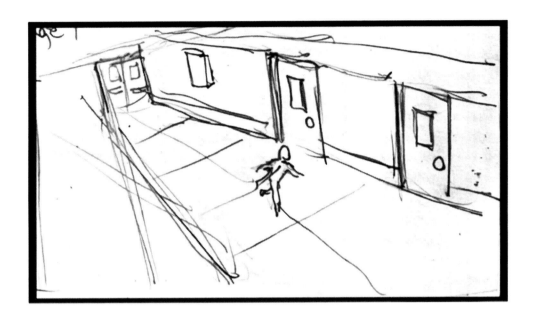

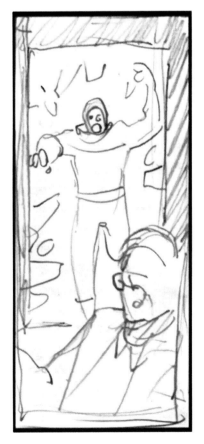

The Motherland Knows
Art by Leandro Panganiban

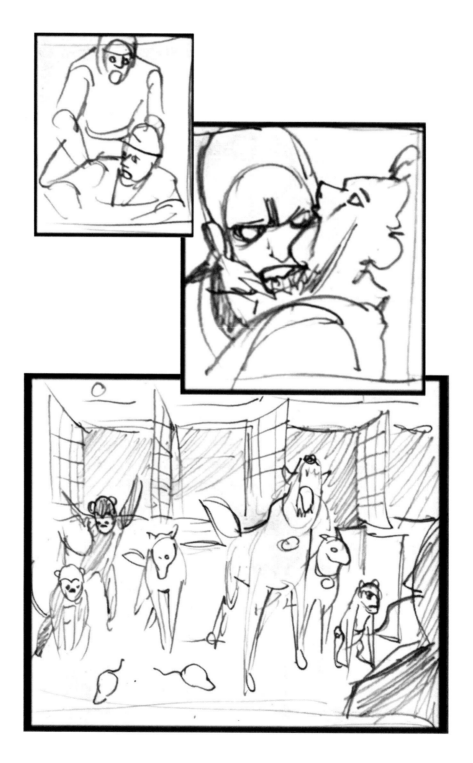

The Motherland Knows
Art by Leandro Panganiban

The Dead & Endless Wastes
Art by Antonio Bifulco

The Dead & Endless Wastes
Art by Antonio Bifulco

CRO
Concept Art by Eric Carter

The Zombie War of 1812
Art by Marc Jameson

The Zombie War of 1812
Art by Marc Jameson

CREATOR BIOS

Rob Anderson

Rob is the writer of *Animal Control: Special Creatures Unit* and *Rex, Zombie Killer*, and the founder of Panda Dog Press (www.PandaDogPress.com). He acted as Project Editor on the first three issues of *Great Zombies in History*. He is also the General Manager of Andy Schmidt's Comics Experience (www.ComicsExperience.com), which offers courses and workshops on comic book writing, art, lettering, and coloring. Rob is based in Virginia and he can be reached at rob@PandaDogPress.com.

Antonio Bifulco

Antonio Bifulco was born in Avellino, Italy. A graduate from the Art Academy of Naples, and a professional artist since 2007, he has been an inker, colorist, penciller, painter, and character designer for several international comic book, card game, and video game publishers. He currently lives and works in Marigliano, Italy, and can be reached at katet2004@libero.it. To see more of Antonio's work, visit fragcomics. deviantart.com.

Eric Carter

A native of Massachusetts, Eric attended the Boston Museum School of Art. There he studied drawing, illustrating, graphic design, and cartooning. Eric has worked on many projects including CD cover art, logo design, and character design for video games and cartoons.

Derek Chase

Derek Chase was born and raised in Indiana before pursuing his career in art by moving to New Jersey. Graduating from the Kubert school, Derek immediately began work with companies such as Elevator Pitch Press, Silent Nemesis Workshop, Clockwork Island, JCE, GameKiss, G-Fan, and many others. His work can be found in horror books such as *The Ultimate Zombie Hunter's Handbook* and *Aliens Among Us*, and in other titles such as *Freestyle* or *Ultimate Dallas*. Still writing and creating art, Derek lives in New Jersey with his partner, Jessie.

Richard P. Clark

Born in a crossfire hurricane (actually Cleveland, Ohio), Richard P. Clark's illustration career began in 1993 while still an undergraduate at the Columbus College of Art and Design. Since then, he's worked for a wildly varied list of clients in several industries– among them HBO, *Playboy*, *The Wall Street Journal* and Alcoholics Anonymous. He's been finding work again in the comics industry — doing some recent jobs for DC, Blind Ferret, Dark Horse & Beyond Reality Media. He lives in upstate New York after a 10-year tour of duty in Brooklyn with his wife, daughter and a goofy dog named Barnaby. You can find out more at his site: www.zippystudio.com.

E.T. Dollman

E.T. is a freelance letterer whose work has appeared in *FemForce* for AC Comics and in numerous independent comic books. You can view his work at www.CaleidoComics.com, and reach him at e.t.dollman@gmail.com.

Eric Drumm

Eric Drumm is a freelance writer hailing from Brooklyn, New York. He has written for such outlets as ToyFare Magazine, Marvel.com and ToplessRobot.com, and has written trade copy for DC Comics. His comics work includes *Tales from the Comics Experience* and *Great Zombies in History*. He enjoys cheeseburgers and Westerns. You can catch him at emdrumm@gmail.com.

Neil Fisher

Neil Fisher is an aspiring writer and educator who lives and works in Frederick, Maryland. He can be reached at fisherneil75@yahoo.com. His work can be seen in *Tales from the Comics Experience*, *Great Zombies in History*, and *Aliens Among Us*.

Paolo Chaz R. Gomez

Paolo is a freelance artist, colorist, illustrator, and animator for hire. You can view his work at www.Paolog.deviantart.com or reach him at Paolochaz_gomez@yahoo.com.

Marc Jameson

Visit "Lost in the Autoganzfeld," the online home of aspiring comic book artist Marc Jameson at autoganzfeld.blogspot.com.

Frederick Kim

Frederick Kim has written for Pocket Book's line of "Star Trek" fiction, and won awards for his non-produced teleplays. He's working on his Big Break, both in comics and Hollywood, in Los Angeles, and can be reached at frederickkim@mac.com. His website is frederickkim.com.

Kevin D. Lintz

Kevin is a former kindergarten teacher, a computer coder by day, a long distance commuter by night, and a comic book nerd on the weekends. kevin@thelaborshed.com

George O'Connor

Along with "Healed," George has written stories for anthologies published by Elevator Pitch Press. He also created and wrote the webseries *664 — The Neighbor of the Beast* (lazyhorde.com) along with over 60 short films. He plays guitar in metal and punk bands. By day, George is a mild-mannered copywriter in the advertising world. He once put a truck on the moon.

Joshua Osborne

An aspiring writer from Central Florida. You can follow him on Twitter @Joshua_Osborne.

Leandro Panganiban

Leandro is a comic illustrator and concept artist based in the Cebu, Philippines. His projects include *The Urn*, written by Patrick Kindlon, *Animal Control: Special Creatures Unit* with writer Rob Anderson, and *Carter Memorial* with writer Brandon Van Hook. His work has also appeared in several anthologies including *The Dead Future* series, *Tales from the Comic Experience* and *Reasonably Priced Comics* to name a few. He can be reached at leandro.panganiban@gmail.com.

Dan Rivera

Dan Rivera lives in Sea Cliff, New York, with his wife, two dogs and a cat. He can be found on Twitter @danriveraprime.

Christian Ruiz

Christian Ruiz is a New Jersey–based artist/designer, Kubert School Graduate, and a generally swell guy. Contact him at http://cjruiz.deviantart.com/

Joe Sergi

Joe is a Haller Award winning author who has written novels, short stories, and comic books in the horror, scifi, and young adult genres. His first novel, *Sky Girl and the Superheroic Legacy*, was selected Best of 2010 by the *New Podler Review*. His website is www.JoeSergi.net.

David Strosnider

David Strosnider is a 1998 BFA graduate of Edinboro University of Pennsylvania, where he studied film, animation and photography. He also spent two rigorous years at Columbus College of Art and Design as an Illustration major. He has been developing stories and characters since he was 12 years old. He can be found at http://strosnider.deviantart.com/

Randy Valiente

Randy is a comicbook writer and artist from Manila, Philippines. More about him and his works can be found on his website: www.randyvaliente.carbonmade.com.

DaFu Yu

DaFu has done interior art for Zenescope (Grimm Fairy Tales, Wonderland Annual) and covers and interiors for Bluewater Productions (Tony & Cleo). He is also the artist on *Rex, Zombie Killer*, and the creator/writer/artist on *MonkeyQuest*, which was a finalist in the Small Press Idol competition. You can see his work at dafuyu.deviantart.com or he can be reached at mqmonkeyquest@gmail.com.

McFarland Graphic Novels

Yellow Rose of Texas: The Myth of Emily Morgan.
Written by Douglas Brode; Illustrated by Joe Orsak. 2010

Horrors: Great Stories of Fear and Their Creators.
Written by Rocky Wood; Illustrated by Glenn Chadbourne. 2010

Hutch: Baseball's Fred Hutchinson and a Legacy of Courage.
Written by Mike Shannon; Illustrated by Scott Hannig. 2011

*Hit by Pitch: Ray Chapman, Carl Mays and
the Fatal Fastball.* Molly Lawless. 2012

*Werewolves of Wisconsin and Other American Myths,
Monsters and Ghosts.* Andy Fish. 2012

Witch Hunts: A Graphic History of the Burning Times.
Written by Rocky Wood and Lisa Morton;
Illustrated by Greg Chapman. 2012

*Hardball Legends and Journeymen and Short-Timers: 333
Illustrated Baseball Biographies.* Ronnie Joyner. 2012

The Accidental Candidate: The Rise and Fall of Alvin Greene.
Written by Corey Hutchins and David Axe; Art by Blue Delliquanti. 2012

Virgin Vampires: Or, Once Upon a Time in Transylvania.
Written by Douglas Brode; Illustrated by Joe Orsak. 2012